CELEBRATING THE FAMILY NAME OF MARTIN

Celebrating the Family Name of Martin

Walter the Educator

Silent King Books
a WhichHead Entertainment Imprint

Copyright © 2024 by Walter the Educator

All rights reserved. No part of this book may be reproduced in any manner whatsoever without written permission except in the case of brief quotations embodied in critical articles and reviews.

First Printing, 2024

Disclaimer

This book is a literary work; the story is not about specific persons, locations, situations, and/or circumstances unless mentioned in a historical context. Any resemblance to real persons, locations, situations, and/or circumstances is coincidental. This book is for entertainment and informational purposes only. The author and publisher offer this information without warranties expressed or implied. No matter the grounds, neither the author nor the publisher will be accountable for any losses, injuries, or other damages caused by the reader's use of this book. The use of this book acknowledges an understanding and acceptance of this disclaimer.

Celebrating the Family Name of Martin is a memory book that belongs to the Celebrating Family Name Book Series by Walter the Educator. Collect them all and more books at WaltertheEducator.com

USE THE EXTRA SPACE TO DOCUMENT YOUR FAMILY MEMORIES THROUGHOUT THE YEARS

MARTIN

In the whispers of time, where history weaves,

Celebrating the Family Name of
Martin

The name of Martin softly cleaves,

Through the echoes of ages, past and gone,

A lineage, steadfast, a legacy drawn.

From ancient hills where old oaks stand tall,

To modern streets where shadows fall,

The Martins walked with heads held high,

Guided by stars in the night sky.

Their roots run deep in soil rich and dark,

Where the first Martin left his mark,

A humble start in a world unknown,

A seed of greatness, long since sown.

In every generation, strength reborn,

From dawn to dusk, from night to morn,

They carried the torch with a steady hand,

A family bound by love's command.

Celebrating the Family Name of
Martin

Through trials that would shake the weak,

The Martins stood, no voice to seek,

For courage was their silent creed,

In every word, in every deed.

The elders speak of battles fought,

Of wisdom gained, and lessons taught,

Of a name that carries weight and pride,

A beacon bright, a trusted guide.

The Martins laugh with a joy so pure,

Their bonds of kinship always sure,

Through tears and smiles, through loss and gain,

They find the sun amidst the rain.

They build with hands that never tire,

With hearts that blaze with inner fire,

Their legacy is not of stone or gold,

Celebrating the Family Name of

Martin

But of stories, cherished, and retold.

From grandmothers' tales by the fireside,

To fathers' advice, a steady guide,

From mothers' care, tender and kind,

To children's dreams, free and unconfined.

The name of Martin is a tapestry,

Woven with threads of history,

Each strand a life, a tale to tell,

Celebrating the Family Name of

Martin

Of hope, of love, where they dwell.

ABOUT THE CREATOR

Walter the Educator is one of the pseudonyms for Walter Anderson. Formally educated in Chemistry, Business, and Education, he is an educator, an author, a diverse entrepreneur, and he is the son of a disabled war veteran. "Walter the Educator" shares his time between educating and creating. He holds interests and owns several creative projects that entertain, enlighten, enhance, and educate, hoping to inspire and motivate you. Follow, find new works, and stay up to date with Walter the Educator™

at WaltertheEducator.com

Milton Keynes UK
Ingram Content Group UK Ltd.
UKHW022012230824
447344UK00012B/730